3-2-1
School Is Fun!

SCHOLASTIC

Children's Press®

A Division of Scholastic Inc.

New York Toronto London Auckland Sydney Mexico City
New Delhi Hong Kong Danbury, Connecticut

Early Childhood Consultants:

Ellen Booth Church
Diane Ohanesian

All rights reserved. Published by Children's Press, an imprint of Scholastic Inc.
Published simultaneously in Canada. Printed in China.

SCHOLASTIC, CHILDREN'S PRESS, ROOKIE PRESCHOOL, and associated logos are trademarks and/or registered trademarks of Scholastic Inc.

1 2 3 4 5 6 7 8 9 10 R 19 18 17 16 15 14 13 12 11 10   62

Library of Congress Cataloging-in-Publication Data

Haley, Amanda.
  3-2-1 school is fun / Amanda Haley.
    p. cm. - (Rookie preschool)
  ISBN-13: 978-0-531-24405-0 (lib. bdg.)   ISBN-13: 978-0-531-24580-4 (pbk.)
  ISBN-10: 0-531-24405-9   (lib bdg.)   ISBN-10: 0-531-24580-2 (pbk.)

  1. Education, Preschool—Juvenile literature. 2. School day—Juvenile literature. 3. Education, Preschool—Activity programs—Juvenile literature. I. Title. II. Title: Three, two, one, school is fun. III. Series.

LB1140.2.H345 2010
371.21 - dc22   2009005498

3-2-1
our school is fun!

We stack blocks
way up high.

Do you think they'll
reach the sky?

Yay! Another day's begun . . .

3-2-1
our school is fun!

It's music time.

TOOT! BANG!

BEAT!

Clap those hands and stamp those feet!

Marching, marching,
one by one...

3-2-1
our school is fun!

YUM, YUM, YUM!

Let's have lunch.

Time to eat . . . MUNCH, MUNCH, MUNCH!

We all like lunch, everyone.

3-2-1 our school is fun!

It's story time.
Let's find a book.

There are lots of stories
in our nook.

We listen till the story's done.

3-2-1
our school is fun!

We finger paint.

RED! GREEN! BLUE!

We finger paint with yellow, too.

Look! We made a yellow sun . . .

Rookie Storytime Tips

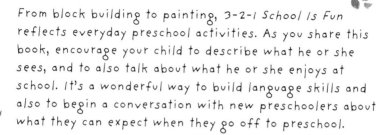

From block building to painting, *3-2-1 School Is Fun* reflects everyday preschool activities. As you share this book, encourage your child to describe what he or she sees, and to also talk about what he or she enjoys at school. It's a wonderful way to build language skills and also to begin a conversation with new preschoolers about what they can expect when they go off to preschool.

Invite your child to go back through the book and find the following things. It's a fun way to build visual discrimination skills.

What's your favorite musical instrument at school?

What is your favorite book?

What do you think these children are building?

What do you like for lunch?

Take turns playing "I Spy" with your child by giving each other clues about things to find on each page!

From block building to painting, everyday preschool activities are fun!

Rookie Preschool keeps pace with eager-to-learn preschoolers! Rookie readiness, science, math, self-concepts, and familiar preschool songs help them learn to read about their world—and the world around them.

This is a My First Rookie Reader.

Tips for LEARNING FUN Inside!

Children's Press®
an imprint of

SCHOLASTIC

$6.95

www.scholastic.com

ISBN-13: 978-0-531-245
ISBN-10: 0-531-245

9 780531 245804

P9-CYL-381